Full Circle

by Kearyn Burke Wynn

For my daughter, Madelyn "Maddie"
And in loving memory of my Nanny and Aunt Margie.

*Their love was a blessing,
this I know is true.
Now I'm giving you my love,
so you can share it too.*

With love and thanks to my family and friends,
whose positive influence has a rippling effect.

From the Illustrator...
For my daughter, Gianna Marie.

AuthorHouse™
1663 Liberty Drive, Suite 200
Bloomington, IN 47403
www.authorhouse.com
Phone: 1-800-839-8640

First published by AuthorHouse   9/2/2008

ISBN: 978-1-4389-0789-5 (sc)

Library of Congress Control Number: 2008907174

Printed in the United States of America
Bloomington, Indiana

This book is printed on acid-free paper.

authorHOUSE®

Full Circle

by Kearyn Burke Wynn

To: Cody

Kearyn Burke Wynn

Life is like a CIRCLE from beginning to end.
As you travel around, be a great friend.

While moving along every bend and curve,
Be kind to your FAMILY, and you'll surely not swerve.

Be SWEET to Grandma, Grandpa, Mom and Dad.

They are the ones you can turn to when you feel sad.

Sometimes your brother or sister might make you mad,
But when you're grown and they're there for you, you'll be GLAD.

Your family may be the easiest on whom you take out your anger.
Just remember they're the ones who will PROTECT you from danger.

If you stray from your PATH and start to be mean,
Your circle becomes broken; believe me, I've seen!

There are so many people you'll meet along the way,
So choose your words wisely, have NICE things to say.

With all of the new FRIENDS that you find,

Never leave your old friends or family behind.

Your circle will be a WONDERFUL place,

If everyone has their own special space.

Each day, each week, and each passing year,
You'll meet new people who in your HEART will be dear.

You may not realize when you meet someone new,
Just how IMPORTANT they will be to you.

BOYS, don't say to the shy girl, "You have *no life*."
One day when you're grown, she might be your wife!

GIRLS, don't leave out the boy who's a bit overweight.
One day when you're grown, he could be your date!

Teasing and laughing are not nice to do.
When someone needs a FRIEND, let it be you.

Every person in this world is BEAUTIFUL in their own special way.

Use your heart to find their beauty, as you travel about each day.

Don't pick on the girl who has bright red hair.
Someday you may forget your lunch, and she will SHARE.

Don't make fun of the boy who's a whiz on the computer.
Someday in COLLEGE, he might be your tutor.

Don't tease the girl
who has a big nose.

Someday she may be the doctor
who can FIX your broken toes.

Don't laugh at the boy who doesn't know the answer and seems "stuck."

Someday he might HELP you when you're down on your luck.

You can't take back the mean things you do,
So start today to become a BETTER you.

Lead by example, tell everyone you meet,

That friends make life's JOURNEY extra sweet.

Making a full circle can be a blast,
Just take your TIME, and don't go too fast.

When your circle is complete, you'll look back and see
That you've given people the greatest gift:

It's fun and it's free!

The best things in life cannot be bought.
With family and friends, you have A LOT.

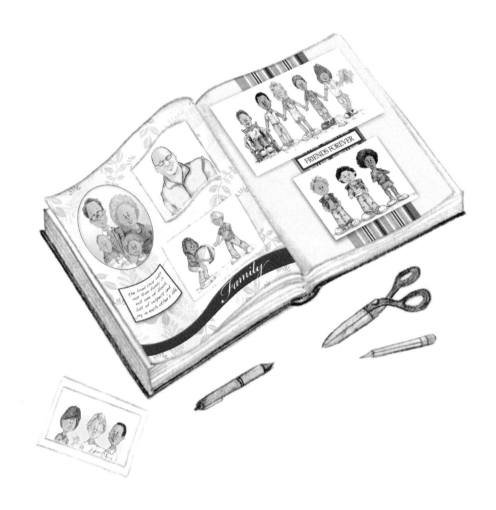

You'll want to be REMEMBERED as "such a good friend,"
Not the *meanie* or *grouch* who never had a hand to lend.

So, each morning when you open your eyes and climb out of bed,
Let these words DANCE inside your head:

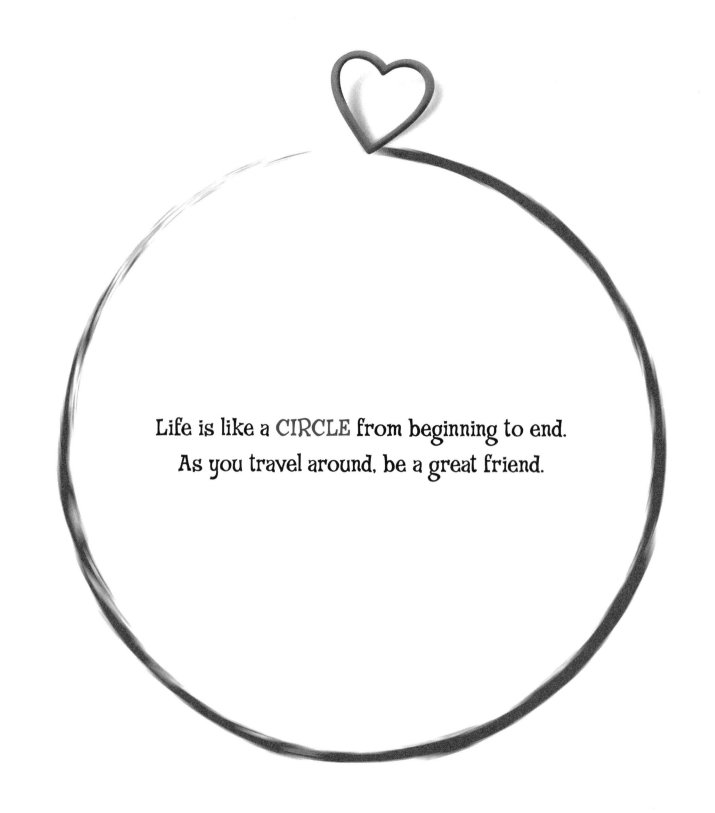

Life is like a CIRCLE from beginning to end.
As you travel around, be a great friend.

Printed in the United States
128335LV00002B